D0930241

Also by Colin Channer

Fiction

Kingston Noir
   (EDITOR)

The Girl with the Golden Shoes

Iron Balloons: Hit Fiction from Jamaica's Calabash Writer's Workshop
   (EDITOR)

Passing Through

Waiting in Vain

Poetry

Providential

So Much Things to Say: Over 100 Poets from the First Ten Years of the Calabash International Literary Festival
   (COEDITOR, WITH KWAME DAWES)

Console

Colin Channer

Farrar, Straus and Giroux : New York

Farrar, Straus and Giroux
120 Broadway, New York 10271

Photograph (details) on pages i, iv, and 123, of the Black Ark Studio ruins,
from Karol Kozlowski Premium RM Collection / Alamy Stock Photo.
Photographs in part II reproduced courtesy of the Providence Athenæum.

Library of Congress Cataloging-in-Publication Data
Names: Channer, Colin, author.
Title: Console / Colin Channer.
Description: First edition. | New York : Farrar, Straus and Giroux, 2023.
Identifiers: LCCN 2023002243 | ISBN 9780374607227 (hardcover)
Subjects: LCGFT: Poetry.
Classification: LCC PS3553.H2735 C66 2023 | DDC 813/.6—dc23/eng/20230130
LC record available at https://lccn.loc.gov/2023002243

Designed by Crisis

Our books may be purchased in bulk for promotional, educational,
or business use. Please contact your local bookseller or the Macmillan
Corporate and Premium Sales Department at 1-800-221-7945, extension
5442, or by email at MacmillanSpecialMarkets@macmillan.com.

www.fsgbooks.com
www.twitter.com/fsgbooks
www.facebook.com/fsgbooks

10 9 8 7 6 5 4 3 2 1

for Senu
for Tubby
for Dub
for Hutchy Bop

Nomadic hearts know there is no rose
waiting at every door . . .

—Jay Wright, "Boleros 9"

Contents

Part II: Hurricane Suite

Part III

Picturebook Brockton

Part IV

Spumante

Weeks diffuse into each other like
they're sprayed. Jetted, they shoot certain:
days, times, doodles, kept appointments
next is lull, pool, fading, flash-disperse.

I was shook and shocked by death,
chanced upon it on a winter walk,
proof of plod for miles behind me
swept in fog, a wet so thick

it blended with the snow that
settled plenty on the sand. It
was not yet daybreak, and I'd driven
miles to walk and think,

find peace in sweat and sea racket,
that ancient wise asthmatic sound.
The light took its lazy time for lifting.
In the shift I saw a darker shaping

than the gray—at two miles a boat
of some proportion, at quarter mile a whale.
Since then I've been lamenting,
moving as if held in gel.

At night I dream it, see it stretched
across the wrack of high tide,
belly to the stars—flung shells and gravel—
throat-part grooved, fins unflappable,

balletic flukes symmetric
in their pointing, how they fused:
all this in half-light, all this in sea dirge,
wet air matte, toned silver,

and I hunched in the hood of my parka,
God-awed before savasana,
stilled as if the glassy eye that looked to me
had fixed me in a century of tintype.

Ah-gah-pay. I've only recently discovered
love of animals—well, Killy, Nan and Rebus,
friends' dogs. Now I've partly taken leave
of language, have given incoherence due.

I know what it's like to be mammal
filled with deepest ocean sounds:
oblivion, solitude, stillness
intermitted by quake roar,

tectonic slipping, lava fissures,
ship propellers drilling,
the human croons of whales.
There is slave in me, fat heritage,

no fluke I'm invested with hurt,
echo of the hunted, located, natural
rights redacted, meagered to resource.
All is flux as I'm collapsing

love and distance, moving through the gel,
my life, edging the canals of my city,
clomping up its hills, memory aerosol,
head in self-cloud, getting Melville

as I should have, watching at him
contemplate the vista from a landlocked house,
hills becoming pods of transmigrating giants:
Greylock. Berkshire range.

There's thirst for music in this less than solid
state. Ampless back in my office,
I knee-prop my Fender, ancient black thing.
Strum it casual, weep;

suck salt in darkness, fingers guessy,
lazing up the sound. Still, something
brusque runs up me: shuddered
wood, that deep flesh shook

that makes string music fuse to you.
The thumbing further breaks the thing in me.
I know what now love is,
know tentative for sure its

incoherence, jelly analog, is mine for life.
The windows stay black and phlegmatic
as the air outside begins to heave with rain.
I hum, thumbing, fashion something of a home,

some succor, pulse quick but steady as I deep dive
to dub. With it comes the baleen
wheeze of mouth organs, plangent blue whoop.
I am dub and dub is water.

Exile, I wish you could have lived in me,
plunging, life *spumante*. I'd slip my hold
on you like magma shot for islands
every single time you breach.

Shunting from Dakar to Casamance

1

A father takes it as his job to order:
rank the powers in the house

so the man o' yard could slice
the crotons with the cutlass

how he gauged it, but couldn't dark his
khaki-wearing self onto the porch;

there, the woman who did pressing
eased a drink to sun from shelter

through the grillwork's diamond gaps,
sumptuous cold water or *bebridge*

but always in glass—for plastic
it was certified held germs

so all like dat deh outside mouth
can't wet-wet people plastic things.

So glass it was or Panther-tasting
water from the hose.

So rank began with who was most
land-close even in a house like ours,

no great design to it: a box of slabs
schemed out on old horse farm

and a bygone orange grove where slavery
kept imagination ligatured

to bias more than law. My father's skin
was pale-beige-watered Scotch.

My mother's blood was part Maroon
she used to boast.

Should kids be embarrassed by
the grown-ups they become?

To us mid in class and tone
our mother's brag said yes,

I was inked wicked, had a story
with an opening in the bush.

Phantom's Skull Cave in comics.
Drive-in newsreels' sunk eyes,

zinc ribs, bloat, tuft hair.
Guerrillas or gorillas at war.

She top-ranked my father, whom
she called in public "dunce police,"

and when he was demoted further
through divorce she just straight-ruled.

Her white tunic made her handsome,
her laughter lit dispensaries and

brought mint coolness to damp wards,
but home she ran it like a capo:

charismatic, loving, then would punch
you if you fucked up like a thug.

If she caught you in a lie she'd
call you to the night porch,

you'd gauge the cutlass-ordered crotons'
silhouette, the argyle pattern grill

then out of air that slow bloom menthol
marking where she slumped.

You trembled when she started:
"Mr. Bitch . . ."

2

How it goes with me—sea calls
and I go to it, not obedient—

with the taut awareness of the archer
who's heard fusillade, bluster call of notes,

or when the cellist looks up,
sees conductor's eyelids droop,

and titivates the bow. It's a string thing,
this hurt, tendon-wound not muscles bound;

and what draws it out of me a little is
the big resilience, ocean of whatever color

cutting itself again and again
salt already rubbed into the wounds.

A posture comes with this witness.
Spine believes it is its doing

but my tendons know. Sometimes they lie
to the ligaments so when I see a boat

way out I feel if I had the pomegranate
switch I used to knot with sisal as a boy,

something sonorous would drain
from a body flung to deck

shocked by whittle arrow on the far skyline
shocked as I was when she'd summon

and for fuckups forgotten
licks would fletch my ass.

3

When I leave her after visits and we
hug in Stamford's near-sea cold

I'm startled always that she's small,
by her skin's flatness—

versus memory, a confusing timbre,
lost sheen tone. The lobby of her pricey

condo is awash with all the foolery
rising tidal every time we meet.

She always says I love you, a habit
picked up on the way to eighty-five.

I'm always struck by change and aging.
On the long drive up the coast

through towns with hope hollowed
linked by some took-for-granted bridge,

I regard with pleasure that endures:
the tall blond grass of autumn;

in winter, fields that float on fog and snow;
summer and the Boston-bound Acelas

on the metal *malecón* between highway
and beach; spring's floral glory,

all New England variegated like
the crotons ordered by the man o' yard

to euphemize the fence. I console
myself sometimes with "pictures,"

her lingo carried over to my home:
Mean Streets, Goodfellas, Gangs of New York,

Scorsese-odes to order, belonging,
violence evangelistic, arch retorts,

dead-body tableaux, virtuosic shoot-outs,
first-chair gunmen in death's chamber,

all those raised neck strings.
When she calls with tender need

to ask if I'm safe how come I didn't call
I dote, wonder if she'll figure how

my not-call is summons, how
once summoned how differently she talks.

Sometimes as she pads from range—
to guest room—our voices echo,

fray as she draws us once again
into the shell she'd been *huxed* from mollusky

in a village by a shore; there, a nameless
river close to where they've built a Sandals now

would gouache an aqua sea. Near there
her squat beige mother

cast her down. "She never love me. Not at all.
She cuss me black."

I knew her. Sister Lyn . . . Miss Minto,
Grandma. Always nice to me.

4

Shunting from Dakar to Casamance
I stopped along a coast, got out,

cocked heels on the hood to get tendons
stretched. I love driving, real driving, stick shifts

and curves and herds of a sudden turning roads
to furry ponds; the unreliability of shafts

and pistons, thus reliance on my ears
to suss which betrayal of bearings, rings

or rods and gears may come.
I inhabit vehicles like a mollusk.

I don't drive cars—I put them on.
Armored, I approach the world.

That time in Casamance I was morose.
In Petit Kassa I'd eaten brilliant

at a café run by whites and guilt
could not console me from

a salad's poised insistent tart,
leaves, some unknown to me,

spooned with unremakable vinaigrette.
All outside the eatery my mother,

shape, skin, hair, smile, low-bridge
nose, slight eyes.

Like the coast of New England,
there were many rivers being seduced

by dreams of being sea and they moved
with purpose for the interview while

mangroves stayed above the drama,
like old heads, just watched.

I stood seaside. Tied pirogues
in front of me were rinds cast off,

bobbling orange, melon, *prongonat*,
as Jamaican pomegranates are called;

beyond this slight armada, vastness
green-blue, collaborating Atlantic westbound.

And I remembered a ska loved by my mother,
a ska by Drummond, "Eastern Standard Time,"

and I recalled a poem I wrote for her,
"Fugue in Ten Movements: Kingston 1955,"

then came visitation from this chat
I'd had with Tommy, Drummond's bredrin

dead now, voice as absolute and present
as a sky unrolls a curtain and it's fog.

Cuban-timbre trombonista used to shuffle
down to placid Kingston harbor

in crepe Dunlops near the prison,
play waltzes with the waves.

And when I thought of this I thought
of how self-harming and the ready-sutures

of the ocean could be scores if I chose so,
scores not settled but turned,

and so it was I found myself at blue
mystery miming Drummond,

an imagined porkpie angled so the brim
was like a far out pirogue's lifting arrowed prow

as I shadowboxed a history and a sea,
a town, a watershed, a continent behind me

as I punched: bag-body heavyweight
or *Jab Jab* doing a jook workout,

Diable, *Diable*, grown-up devil boy.
On the road to Ziguinchor,

I thought why Mum loved Drummond.
Did she hear that cello-sorrow in his tone?

How Long Could I Have Been Weightless?

After the smooth up-pull the car dove fish-efficient
in the tractor-trailer's wake. By then the thick wheel

cuts had tapered down the long, curved grade then vanished,
leaving undulations in the drifts.

All the way from Montreal through French-toned
Vermont we'd held to, mostly all alone,

through nighttime Massachusetts, the Berkshires
rhythmic now, the rise and fall of roadways

lung-like, up and down, the black outside squelching
with each splat. The snow fell lazy-seeming

but the mass had force to it, a will thrust like those
of sea currents, and in the down rush the car's

back end began to flex. The side-muscling
came in series, ripples, quivers, pulse,

and I was in it countersteering while
the coffee spilled in the careening

into through and out of what the frost-dimmed
lights could see: all murk then,

the whole world untrustworthy, murk and
splat, and splat and speed, and ridges:

the rudder backlit by dials,
the fingers and their grips

the road itself a reef and I was skidding, skidding,
tread and road unbonded into flight.

How long could I have been weightless?
Does it matter now?

I reach now to recall what flew by me:
trees in kelp shadow, gelid embankments

snow shoals, formations of a world
so much like ours, just under water,

glimpse of where we're headed
by degree.

Four wheels on the snow again,
clutching, shifting, easing down

compression bracing on
momentum's rush I saw it:

deep snow swashed in fan pattern
to the breadth of the road

the white rig turned over,
red stamp on the side of

it: strike of harpoon. What fluke
of luck had saved me? Which flake

launched me to air/water,
racing my breathing, slowing me down?

Lent

I mount a crest in coffee country and it's Oregon.
In all directions, ridges saw the Caribbean out of view.
In these wet mountains, clichés of the tourist

board elapse, beach fables die famished,
palms straggle, get left behind as pine and casuarinas
gather up in bamboo lushness with the blue mahoe.

I'm backpacked like a turtle, urgent-slow—flat-footed,
flippered in caricature, years after the surgery
and the knees just not the same, but why am I

sloshing fact with expectation—age is desiccating,
cartilage fails—and why confabulate? In this wet-air
ecotone before the clouds dismiss the fog and claim

the forest green is dense as smoke. At this height
the roads from Kingston show themselves:
escaped undressing runaways: tarmac, gravel, track,

and I sense ahead of me oblivion in the green-absorbing
white-gray silver, the clouds among the roots of trees
a shifting wisping thing. I'm elated and embarrassed.

Seeing relations of what ought to be disparate
is my living, my burden, my habit, my gift.
I left this island early, never learned to love with value

in my language, my fishes, my birds, my trees,
and as I do without my contacts, I see what's there
but not apparent, sense essence, trace travels,

overdubbing—map. In this way I'm kin to semiliterates,
brother to naïfs. Error-maker, I navigate on faith.
Small point: none of these trees are native. Like,

well, *me*, in the generic, they were brought. And as I
inch here in self-cloud wrapped in dense wetness that's actual,
glimpsing every now and then a farm—coffee bushes

with red dottings swerving with awareness
of the contour lines (said farm always well-terraced),
I imagine what it must have meant

to be a bringer, one gifted with the say to make a cut,
a shift, a graft, a cauter—suggesting by decree as interrogative:
"What if we bring *this* from there and make it grow *here*,

and transport it *thusly* so I can have more comfort in my
part-time home?" Mist, deep forest (and too much Walcott, frankly),
have a way of making poets fantasists (infantilists?) of exile.

I left is all, and swiftly. Now I know no birds by shape or color,
sound or season, silhouette or ceiling of flight, or what fruit
bears in what season, except in New England where I live.

What does this make me? I've never lived on
the West Coast much less Oregon, but those hills
I walked beyond Portland called me home to here,

these arabica mountains draped in mist, cloud covered
as though modest, where creeks occur as sound, pulling
me to Sahel travels, to courtyards marked by mud walls,

spume fountains; to heard-of women veiled. Here,
hip shapes form out of rustle, Kromanti women
ghost from shadow, ghillie-plumed a century plus

from patient self-erasure from the force of busha's pen;
here where slaves reconstituted, made war and news
by raids from hidden passage, from quick-effacing trail,

I know each aqua pool gyrates below the river's
urgent silver—blatant—but I don't. I understand the colonizer,
get the substandard with an inkling a promotion lay elsewhere

perhaps-feasibly-conceivably-perchance;
share the dubious heritage of gaze, of making all before me
what I want, gating my imagined, seeing me in everything,

accosting landscapes and handing them confessions,
making them my subjects, what I study, but in that childish style
(ask my profs at Hunter), without diligence, eliding grains,

compressing essence: touché, Bennett: colonizing in reverse.
The remix is dub's premise. Reggae conquers. Not maybe actual.
But it's how it sees the world. There is more to say on this.

All I know is beyond these mountains is a Portland,
a whole parish with beaches in soft valleys classified
from day-trippers to the hills, banks of white sand umbrellaed

by ferns, cataracts with chromatic pools, slim and subtle falls.
A poet said, and please don't quote me, that travelers
are the last arrivants—like soft waves they come with sorrows;

we regard them, then they come with conquest . . . you.
I am, and I am not. I accept this. But I don't.
I am that I am I am I am I am. This is Tosh.

Spear jooks: *My way is so long, so long, but the road is foggy, foggy.*
Who am I to question these prophets, men who took the time
to know the names of trees and herbs, which fishes schooled

in what season, air pressure's augury—odd migrating of birds?

Mostly Hamburg, 1972

(for and after Kwame Dawes)

Confusion is the foreigner's advantage. Natives
tamp the nuance in their sounds. Stranger
seeking refuge pockets vowels, picks gesture,
learns body, gets caught up on the cobble
slang of shoes. The polite in this tram-knit
city far from English smile quick
but their toes? Uneasy. Hump leather. Squeak.
A Channel boat and hyphenated rolling stock
from London, and London from his ackee trees
an iron bird away, he practices in silence as he walks
the bird-flecked squares, tweed hat on his half-dread
'fro at bias, murmurs new songs, scatters wild
consonants that roost now in his mouth.
In empty churches that stood firm while getting dusted
by bomb-plumes one turns easy to infinity and origin,
to how some children if god-blest just have
it natural: organ pipes. Halfway to Rasta
but so wayfarway from home, prayer becomes
a little easy, comes to him organic-like
where beer has names like *Weizen*,
starts to anchor in this place where
no one (yet) says *nigger*, but the bread
will chop your mouth; and there's been months of this,

two seasons, time the sweaters swagged in
sticky Kingston serve. Reggae masters dress
up cold to say they travel, but what circumnavigates
is just their songs, lyrics that betray, go abroad
with promise as to Panama, but only drabs return.
Muddle is the foreigner's advantage.
With slow talk and hand signals, pictures poked at
while spotting needle in the groove,
I play LPs from my satchel for the curious,
drink what they bring deeply, watch
them smiling, feeling jokified by how
they clap their brows, not to what is sung
exactly, just the loosey-tighty sound:
Wilson Pickett, Marvin Gaye, Sam Cooke,
and me in and with the whole of them
just riddim different swung. Once, in my bedsit
I watched eyes die and nose holes enliven,
twitch as mysteries in the soulcase were wooed
and I was wheeled back to my grandfather's
cement church near Dungle,
eight and speechless from mama water broke
and two doves clawed my epaulets; I was
lifted as I sung in what said some was Latin,
others said was normal clap-hand tongues;
but what it was it was, and what it was came rapid,
flocks of fire black and silver lifting from my throat
and I could see their sound make patterns—yes,
a vision shook me. To see sounds above a praising

congregation shape one way quite certain then quick-shift
like soldiers on a dress-up march or shine starlings—
(Know those small, black birds?)—that's a mystic,
and so, all the way from mento, ska, doo-wop, and rocksteady
into this here catapultic time I sing from mystic,
even my love songs—them is mystic, mystic mix with soul,
so no producer can predict me, no chord can bind me
for I can quick-change where my music goes.
Dear Lord, what wrong have I done thee, why did
you change your heart? Why did you blight
thine own promise? How many songs must your servant
sow before he reaps? I hold steadfast while
others sing less tuneful, demand sparse brasses,
bleat righteous, eat calabashes full of Ital then
rehearse the hunger-sound. As these stained saints
gaze down on me I am bilious, broken, broke.
Even minor reggae masters know the ginnal roots of myth,
know to make it seem natural, ever-there—adventitious—
that rehearsed amalgam: prince royal, prophet, pimp;
and so he goes about his days singing softly as if unto
himself, marking the squares, consoling lindens
on the tram-keloided streets, trailing that silk smell
of soul music like the fighter-pilot scarf he likes to wear,
the throat language coming slow-no-itching
as he gives his neighbors greetings, but he still scouts
out their feet; friendly, but in character standoffish,
screw-face, naw-beg-nutten-from-nobaddy.
How we say *aloof*.

Dub

What I've come for in the house of dub
is cotched up in a corner, black and dented.

Through the dust that fogs it, slashes
where the faders used to be. The half door

claps; smells douse: old damp,
goat fur, guano, bats. The roof holes

mate the algae puddles; loss amalgamated
has clung. Hear me now and hear me good:

to shake dubroyal's console,
watch insects slush from it in seeped ocher,

feels at once minute and big, pint epic;
impulse comes to clean it, pay some vague penance,

or pray. The half door pries itself open;
there's wind rush as I note make—

student always—dun mattresses, dead leaves,
hen bones in slack boxes, a wad of condoms

going resin with each day. All this looked to
while I aggregate, re/aggregate, or try to,

what was here when *him bruk up* music,
made mash-ups, loopy instrumentals

flecked with chant snatches, fogged horns,
stridulant insects and echo, mountain ranges

hazing, far-repeating hills; these were my blues,
my hymns, my war songs, my lay psalms

in the epoch of *pantslent*, vicious Nixon,
Indira's starlet shades and what they promised;

DJ Castro live remixing history; Marley's ambush;
arson at the old-age home, 150 golden ladies

burned—mass grave for their remains like
charred idols—the Cold War hot and local,

tribal killings like the Irish, gunmen
green and orange culling more in months

than all the Troubles, the melodica our bagpipe,
roots chanter, source of skirl, its sketching eerie,

chalking on the B side for the black exquisite corpse.
What I've come for—I leave.

Bubble

Love from another time beneath me
in that new white cube house, mouth-water
from my brother's lip a dollop on my arm;

and the bed irks when he fidgets
in the wait-for-signal from the gap
between floor tiles and the ground;

not "the grounds" . . . ground . . . house bottom,
hush wilderness where short
unpainted pylons bear our house,

moral interstice of lizards, worms
and insects—where with keyholes
in our milk teeth we go crawling

with jook sticks to kill;
but not today, not now, not in this
drowsy interval, not with bellied

dog beneath us filled with pups;
expectant anguish, feels like Advent
service at St. Mary's or the held-in

glee on card nights near Christmas
when big people leave red punch
with anise to the ferns and tip to Mum's

barracks and we hear the rip of tape
in plastic sleigh beds getting pulled,
and we guess at gifts;

so, me and Gary sleepy-tangled-up this morning,
birth funk rising from the privates
of the house; *peeny-wally* dust makes

helix in the light the louvers plane;
the pregnant dog sounds settled in the place
where she belongs, the crawly gap,

our dim far-fetching range,
and in bed my mind gallops,
my chewed fingers work, names coming

as I pick tufts from the blue chenille
we cover with, our inner sky, thought bubble,
holder of our wishes, gases, pissings,

bun crumbs, Milo, condensed milk,
the drowsy pleasure of being above new
life as it's ushered in not lost on me,

not lost because it's just too big to grasp;
this is six-year-old bare love,
just adorable distress as each

pup imagined is named, my mind alert
for big dog bray or jostle, or a sightless
infant chirp, and now it comes!

newborn's here-in-wonder cry on waking
in an outtabelly underworld;
the next sound comes to mind still

when I think *efficient*—
one growl all slaughtered runts,
and every time I hear the sound

and every time I hear the sound
and every time I hear the sound
the sound the sound the sound . . .

Oreja

Given time, I'd know the word,
but had I not done duty,
sight unseen agreed
to take Alberto's *madre* on a walk
I would not have learned the clave
beat of boots and Roman sandals
on our stone canal.

Blood beat, it stayed reliant
as a dog or cast shadow,
this sound of middle life unleashed,

and we rambled arms looped in summer's rush wind,
purposeful as migrants but willfully naïve,
navel-gazing neovatics
acting like tense did not matter,
like what-next was up to belief.

Sun-stunned by August Providence,
bruised town west from where Cape hooks brawl sea,
we moved in shook cloth, hair masque
and skin attar to the brink,
left downtown—sought art.

From the hump-emplaced museum
we looked down. Light slighted.
Canal turned zip in gathered frock
flung off.

By then discussion was finished.
I'd been humbled, embarrassed,
Spanish sputtered when Caracas came up.

Oh, wrecked Caracas,
Bolívar's sinking galleon,
Chavismo's glowing tanker run aground.

The museum was chilly.
We caught breath in its smug café,
sat thigh-thigh, spangling
leftists bereft,
sipping thoughtful—tea then staring
past the basement of our cups.

Would know the word in time,
but if I'd not said yes to my friend,
gone for that walk,
in language made some rough wrong turns
I would not have been there
feeling tender to texture's proletariat,
the millions of slighted small words.

Started with redundance; Ana María indulged,

eyes / *ojos*
eyebrows / *cejas*
lash / *pestaña*

I see her face on teacups now.
She taught *tazas* don't have handles.
In Spanish cups have ears.

Console

Now, the Grundig in this dealer's window
screaming, the silent oval speaker like a Munch,
and I hear it on a Sunday as I best recall:

that bathroom in that prefab, that trick of cupping
water in that comrade season, darkness
a must without power, the add-on

for cook and cleaner capping the louvers for life.
Could have been then, mid-divorce's tamarind season
when we felt so damn boxed in:

Charles and Phyllis split but still unioned
in our young range-finding minds. Perhaps.
Could have been the year we moved

with our mother, took pause down plain,
too close we children felt to homes
with legs and shingles, decks with iron rails,

none of this Georgian—just old,
just wood smell, just cellar,
just rafters with no clothes

and we were moderns—could have been
that year. What's sure is I was kneeling,
plump pink-soaped and worried,

facing a pipecock struck dumb.
Half offering could buy cut cake,
just farfetching. For sure my thoughts were heard.

I whispered *godforgiveme godforgiveme*
then it came—the hiss, soft come-on
from some near but distant district,

and I prayed in precognition
of the what's-to-come,
the *chek*-anticipating *boff,*

the crawl in dust
and coiling up to ackee bough
of what should not be Sunday heard.

I spat in my hand middle
tried to streak Palmolive off
agitating/agitated, guilt unconsoled,

and nothing from the faucet.
Riddim surged.
The rest of that moment? Lost.

Mutton legs? Grown out.
Greed? Still work. Now, this
dark wood record changer,

belly for the LPs flat and good.
In a tree lit with pods red like apples,
that thing I heard that day,

Tannoy of the dubman,
white steel flared long throat.
Maquette, serpent skull and jaw.

2

Uh luh luh luh, peculiar kissing, tot-felt synesthesia,
scent of long hellos and shade of pink
that made a helix in the mouth,

weird but not wrong those tongue greetings,
good shocks they'd bring, Pentecostal shivers
and stoic Anglicans we were.

Now here at Nurse's column *uh luh luh luh*
palming scabbed enamel on her noon-hot gate,
warping thing lock-heavy like a Paris bridge.

Nurse needs help with her toddle.
Basil odor leads her from the shade, and she comes
in patient revelation: skin like her crotons,

face cross-sectioned cabbage rose.
To me I'm no strange arrivant
but reliably myself,

boy who hustled hug-ups
from his mother's friends.
Uh luh luh luh.

She asks if I'm the chap
who brings the thyme.
It's not owed to anybody—

being recalled.
Uh luh luh luh. Incoherence.
Lurking music in the mouth.

3

EMDR: Take 1
It's the episode of dengue where the boy
lay slumped on daybed soaked,
and I'm with him on the back porch,

fanned by breadfruit leaves.
Chained ferns circle, as would pyrotechnics
some plume.

A word comes. *Frowsy*. Remembrance
seeps out seventies' scents,
rum liniments, stewed lights,

cook-down liver, place mats (vinyl),
album sleeves (cardboard),
horse shit crumbed in clay pots

dimpled with thumbprints.
At sundown dyed horizons,
skirls of passing peanut smoke.

I'm gone, the boy marooned.
Detach is what was asked before
my ears were muffed with Bose.

And so it was I could console
my me not me, my was that was
so meagered, marooned,

and turn as Gilgamesh from
fade/dissolve/ing Enkidu
struggling to breathe.

4

My mix has always been comedic,
what occurred told absurd
as if to match the age's flares and fringes,

slant berets, patch pockets, Jesus sandals,
unembroidered guayaberas, suede chukkas,
reggae, afros, dreads.

Once in bed I snuffled. There was good dub on,
moody, atmospheric, songs grinding
on themselves till flotsam, echo, echo,

everything afloat, as if Tubby's
ghost was organizing from history's
bass bottom, history, history, sea.

Another time in Narragansett,
a winter. Puppies frisking off leash.
I had the urge to walk behind

them, mash up patterns.
I said okay I'll tell,
but, my funny may/could

come forth tragic,
and Nurse sad drinker
made Humbaba myth.

5

EMDR: Take 2

There's a hint of tryst in their
meetings, man, woman, couch,
chair, her necklace from Tibet,

gray cascade, fugue music,
incense, low lights.
He feels awkward if he's early

and another is there.
He keeps coming though
he's skeptic,

skeptic though her method has initials
plus a name. He just knows
her skin has crimps

near cleavage.
She takes tea with butter
when he dreams.

On Sugar and the Carnival of War

At-sink coffee;
way horizon curry lined.

We're spilling turbinado
as we spoon out in half-light.

Jouvay. Sugar the jute-frocked assassin
is clumsy, carries *shekere* and crunch,

disarms with hemp smell.
I know *alluvial*, but if not

I'd sense the crystals' origin in earth,
lava over eons going crumble,

sawyer negros ganging timber—
clearing—language will and

muscles breaking down.
In the show framed by sash window

clumps of palms stickfight,
get limber in *gayelle*, fronds as long *bois*

spinning, blurred. A fruit of some size
falls out there in shadow

and we can't see what's destroyed,
what ant pounded

what twig maligned.
We perk in hush

as what happens in filial dry climates
when drones do their work

and *boof* thoraxes dismembered.
Of a sudden   collateral gone.

I took my coffee black today.
Somewhere without degreed baristas

near-blind hand inchworms
a counter and

the crystals' ant-attracting
frass is dulled of bite.

Pain's absence is a danger.
Blindness of the spirit a choice.

Notes on a Minor Prophet

1

Sheared, roof-gone, charred walls blue as when
they warrened took-in people called at
from the crate he preached from in his slum;
all palm-armed and neck-veined, scissors knotted
to his sash, he quoted reggae for the relevance,
mimed cowboys as he shrieked of mounting demons,
a goat kid tethered to his ankle often
as a promise for a feast—nyammings at his rampart,
that place there on that rise there at that lane-end
trimmed with noise and mud cloth returned as rivers
in a vision's flat perspective caught in fowl blood,
revenants, waving sheets of zinc.

2

Him spin-the-rolling in the dirt yard, leaping,
waist of flamed air; he's a far but near god's sublimate,
and all the shango drumming of the took-ins
in their cream robes and skin balm camphor-redolent
incite rewilded chickens to whir, birds as wigs flung off,
and some boys my age at roost in almond trees
bend from their balcony, clap louder than

the copperleaf applause, hooting at Pukumina,
what a poppyshow! and me on the back porch,
still short pants, breath-caught holding meds for his pressure—
mum waiting in the Escort, chilluming Rothmans
in that Savlon-smelling white dispenser's shift—his art!
the porch a berth of easels, primed canvas, hardboard dense
with torqued bodies visioning floods and pus eruptions,
portraits of orgies, lips wry but eyes astonished,
Jesus and the disciples as a Jonkanoo band: horse head,
belly woman, pitchy-patchy, devil, cow head, and them
small shells, and coffee beans applied, outlining,
all done clumsy but with purpose to kid thinking,
the difference perplex; through the grillwork,
dust misted, veiling all except a turban's tossing boat.

3

Then the Bronx years, college, a summer, the van ride there,
the chambers heaving-dropping with the breath of rescued lives,
the orchard of spat seeds and outlaw pissing cooling the roof
as we reasoned on that chuckup porch in gesso scent
and chicken necks in cornmeal frying crisp: and no
he'd never heard of Basquiat, but had seen New York
by star travel, had never sailed or flown, but
seen the world . . . *oh truly? when you first see my*
painting-them, fright take you? you know when me scare?
when time me see the book that show the plan,

how everything on those ship was neat like burial suit,
well measure, maths out perfect, drawmetry;
from that day I stop buy egg a shop—every time
I see the box I see the damn cross-sected ship; when me cut pawpaw
long way me give a bless to every seed.

4

As well, the limp he hitched with in his sick days,
two strokes down, the paintings counterratic color warps
of sliced fruit; whir color; color war; tint ambush,
the paint impastic with scabs he picked off,
piss pot by the easel beaded Haitian with ants;
in the dirt yard lumped with gold almonds
a cast pot on coal thyme fumes the good
of goat head soup; remember this,
catch it as it was.

Unconsoled

In some language somewhere there has to be
a word that means *melancholicallybewildered*,
an anfractuous set of glottals, slipping vowels
like a counterwailing helix of wet stone stairs.
Somewhere the carping of a tool against a whetstone,
a held note that trails to hush, and a wether ram
tied to a stump marks time, padding,
hooves morsing out a stutter. Feast eve.
This may be the genesis in every language—
some sentience suspended in desire for the known
and knowable comfort of violence willed against it,
this wrath a sure hurt planned for, looked to,
the elision from this, this, *wanting*, to flight
or free fall nothing but a blurred uncertain
versus slaughter in the solid hitch to post.
The first scat I know of shot in Genesis, a bleat-letting
in Eden and what an erasure, no mention
of the animal, only that the maker slew,
drew blade cross cello tendons
and involuted gasping curdled, flesh made shit and notes.
So much on my conscience, Chet on the Grundig,
Davis on my mind, the distance
in imperial measure to New York

from East Saint Louis lesser but more long
than those kilometers to Paris, town of gray stone
where a lover called his voice *le sable*;
queased him till he saw it meant sand.
Seams beveled, Davis cotches in that slack
un-army posture on the dream-lit auction stage,
couples in the smoke dark murking,
red glows with wispings—haint eyes.
Second set and Rob Roy loose, he wills that small hall bigger,
fashions for his comfort first a cable then a mic.
Fear in four chambers, he's stasis; acoustic he hovers,
leans backward held by history in the interstice
of fall and flight, *melancholicallybewildered*,
sentient but abstracted from the world,
in and over his own parable,
shudder in his gut; the notes come in pellets
staccatting, stutter-staggering, man, god and goat,
his own twisting entrails too wet to think of as
sure rope. In some language somewhere,
there has to be a word that means
melancholicallybewildered. Sure.

Roots

Then, the future was glaucomic, the bore through mangrove
in the dugout slow. I recall the water in its color tannic.
I see now an olive wake dissolving from the churn work
of the screw. A time would come—it seems it has—
to redecipher, understand again the meaning of the motor's
open vowels louding up a sacred space.

Corporal Pitt, the bully, said something far beyond himself,
"You see all what favor frame for madman basket?
Those are aerial roots." He pointed and we took
his reedy finger as command, us six good recruits—
cadet acolytes joined for camping life—and paused
eye-sweep for crocodiles.

I plait time to those wetlands often. To be black where
I live now is to bivouac. White is wilderness in all seasons.
I carry *bankras* of one-one sorrows; gods in a haversack of joy.

Out on long lug-sucking walks through marshes south of Boston,
close-west fairly of the Cape, I wink "like" to the look of bulrushes,
how they call to bible Moses, kinda favor sugarcane.
Who resists the cattails' saucery?—such flirts—but the names.

Little Massachuck. Sachuest. Sapowet.
Say them soft; no, shout these native names,
names of the plowed near, and housed to,
the made margin, the selvaged by road,
the done to as America tends to do with indigenes,
its what-it-failed-to-kills.

At water's edge a man in waders arcs a lure; snaps it
out for bass. Tammed women with clam baskets hunch
against a pushy breeze in group leverage. Seashells smaller
than the ears of newborns crunch in the wake of boots.
My dry-meniscus knees go *skurch* on pebble shoals.

Sinuous chapel festooned-gaudy, by ibis candlelit,
I sight you, but how I coulda note full conscious
your low-key frieze of halophytes, the mangroves' gazing
wall of afroed saints? I was just man-youth.

Once, I pilgrimed to another coast of my island
to be witnessed to in soulcase by the final two
      uncaught unkilled sea cows,
figures so of there, but as their wakes were, evanescent.
They're gone now like the Arawaks as I too must go.

I go. Home for now to Providence. Comb-somed,
bearded, chukking old Bean boots—apparently adaptive.
Every hair a root.

The Fat Man
Spoke of Fish

The fat man spoke of fish,
only he was drawn,

head shaved athletic,
rug beard cleaned up,

outfit black,
New Yorkish,

metal specs selected,
not got.

His précis—feria. *Dónde?*
Nicaragua. Portion, *extra grande*

doble! A *guapote*, lake-lurking
bully dealt with wicked,

scored and salted. Battered.
Taught its tender side.

Fit man spoke of flaked
flesh, then called for veggies—

well, for veg-adjacents:
hummus, falafel, baba-frigging-

ghanoush. No sheet of pita.
Was that shiver, lack of comfort

in the tight back booth?
His two new still-fat friend-dem

nyamming chicken,
probing beef lobes.

Stew juice gouached
rice bowls.

New friends listened, sipping.
Water, Turkish coffee,

Gilbey's gin. Followed reminiscing
to gist: flesh missed.

Old friend, me, barely fit-ish,
eyed bread, impatient

as my once-fat friend fed muse.
I ate soup with good mouthfeel—

and with relish,
turned *alabanza* for oil,

for cumin—for the give-in
to the blade by lamb fat,

for what I peppered: questions,
details. Town?

Granada. When?
A year, what the fuck.

With notes I'll do duty:
dream fish deep-fried

the way the ex-fat man
spoke of it, his whale.

Take the vegan's torture
off his mind.

The Fixed Mutability
of Things

Heft!
Book-thick comic. Spectacular fat.
Graphic marvel scaled up like
ghost novels, sword sagas,
and that serve-me-long adventure
with the Greek who killed wicked,
    jookjook
     daggerdagger,
ginnal pest of giants
who tried corking caves with stone.

Heft!
A dim bookshop in Kingston,
brick and lumber district near the port.
Then, comics and labor were thin.

Above the door a sign,
    no reading was allowed.

The lone clerk by the looking case
creased napkins for his nape,
shift to damp from paper privilege being soon.

He watched at me, sole custom,
from the asham dust on everything,
the only one in days.

Settled enterprise, temple to loss, I swept it. With gaze:
maps, globes,
fainting stacks of *Life* and *Look*,
cards in biased carousels,
wet encyclopedias,
ink but no pens,

and a beat-up thing that would have been
a silent platen press.

Beside it, trimming's implement,
the cutlass reconcocted
to dissemble field work.

Inside, something fixed was cracking.
Mutable came in swarm of feel, not word.

Heft!
In this his world I had it.
I held it skinned it
let transparent plastic flop my shoes.

Bedazzled

*Burro Banton a di only veteran artist that go Europe and
open the festival and close the festival. Him get two pay.*
—Peter Metro, dancehall legend

Air an instrument of the tongue.
—Robert Pinsky, "Rhyme"

Hearing Burro trace the sky in couplet,
the mic from Nicodemus arming
boom re-arming hand to hand,

I began to *ribbi-bang, bong-widdly*,
find giddy in the sounds of dead books—
so *eftest* and *cock-a-hoop* amused me,

good nonsense like *slang-dang*; and
every Dolby-short cassette respooled by
pencil *foxship* made school-ordered scansion drum.

That Elizabethans rode riddim, bedazzled,
and the work turned pay itself,
at night, parts assigned soft-said

downstage uproof my warm flat white scheme-house,
the almond tree backdropping, a streetlight key,
slang-dang and *foin* pop out of me.

Redoubt

The board was cotched in a corner,
black and dented
through the dust that fogged it,

slashes where
the faders used to be.
Wind. The bubbled half a door

behind me shut and I was
caught in webs of smell,
damp heat,

nebulizing piss,
herb ash,
guano,

junjo puddles.
Loss amalgamated clung.
The roof appeared

bombed by pomegranates.
Through the punch holes
spotty looks at orchids,

mossed branches,
long vines falling loose.
Prongonats I self-corrected,

no pomegranates here.
Uncorrupt the word
dubmaster had commanded

from this hideout in the hills:
Uncorrupt it, sound it,
make redoubt.

To the vines I added
endings: Scully, Helios, Ampex, Shure,
closed my eyes and delved in testing,

wondering if a lucid dream would come.
No prize for being pilgrim
but the steepness of the walk,

until on leaving for a moment
I was him, and saw things clearly,
board as when he'd made it.

Tu'n over the system. When
in doubt, redoubt.
How good and pleasant

it would've been to know
that mad hermetic world,
that snow globe take-two version

in the bush all that bass shooking,
watching reverb units
flung to blast.

They said he eq'd mics
for *squallie*, relished hunger's ashy
liftoff from the mouth.

Suffer was a genre,
keening took into his console
then put out.

II

Hurricane Suite

Acts 8:26–40 in Dub ("Ask for What You Want")

Cause although it's windy not warm
Jah will guide us through the storm
—Gregory Isaacs, "Storm"

Hunch is the posture of the poet.
We don't stack proof in integers like
spines or wood ricks. A gap?
We fill it, feel it, intuit I guess.

Was it Benjamin? *The camera introduces us to*
unconscious optics. McLuhan right? *We become*
what we behold. Who am I out of/within
this scene of benediction? Should I ablute/lament?

Back two thousand years and change in Gaza,
wilds where sand was sea, a careful Ethiopian
moored his chariot, sipped on the bloodscript of Isaiah,
reggae's ranking prophet, till Philip sent by hunch

from Jerusalem drew down, actsed the man
if he could smell and taste the words.
Said the seed-free plant of Candace:
Who does the prophet speak of? Another or himself?

Philip poured the eunuch drafts of Jah's promise. *And as they went on their way, they came unto a certain water, and the eunuch said, See, here is water: what doth hinder me to be baptized?*

Tetto

The flat roof is
filled with folks
as if it's drinkstime.

Woman with
dark tresses presses
damp against a ledge

sloe-eyeing
Providence!
—Can it be?

She makes it Venice.
Flotsam? Flotilla.
Fear? Reason.

Leaping? Flight.
—Wayfarway
from home.

Eye

Mist and drizzles turn to buffets then
all normal snaps from roots,
havoc sent to ravage wave to wave.
So it was for Wampanoag, Nipmuc,
Niantic, Pequot, Narragansett—
deluge-colonizing, gust insults,
bodies shook like canoes in crosscuts,
pneumonic fear, and the drowned boy's
last view—the eye—what stillness.
One new god's promise. Peace.

Bunch

We throng on the steps to the tide.
So our great-grands did on docks,
capstones of courses from hamlets,
towns loved on by always-leaving
winds, damn nomad scoundrels—
Tramontane, Cierzo, Gregale.
Oh, to herd at tide with ardor,
sails full of faith, good at hunching,
herb-intimate fingers trade-brilliant,
this country's limits unlearned.

We gaze Town Sea made sudden,
the fable of a car-roof shoal.

Providential archipelago of grief
in which a Mayan god, fellow migrant,
stages monologues in cross dialectics
—breezes wild but ordered, shifting
right to left—how do I depart?

Someone—who knows?—stutters a novena.
We together mumble-whisper *bluhbluhgod*,
accents shifting, blown of course toward

the willed-to-be-forgotten pitch of English
waffled by our great-grands, tongues flecked with
known shame-bearing words, argots of bias,
blessings, caste worship—chant, spell, hex.

Grandma's grit language. Blind the evil eye.

The Sea and
Its Creatures

Cousin from Praia, fellow islander,
war fragment, *grogue* me
as this shot of cars
in flood dissolves to whales.

For this is what binds us here,
the sea and its creatures.
Islands mark limits, hem shore.

Lavish recognizer, comer
from a stranded necklace off
the Guinea coast, your kin made
comfort in Nantucket's parable,
relied on song and salt for ease,
salt smell ambition's analgesic,
crystals healing what migration
gutted, fish by fish.

From those who came before
you learned Aquidneck:
marshes, coves and harbors,

winds that go still of a sudden
then like whale spear
or *morna*, death-tinge plunge.

Guinea remnant, I slave blood.
All England took was "new"
so, I citizen. No shaft nor barb
in I conscious. There's reggae,
Jonah, whale. It's with them
I myth travel. The math of hunting
proves blunt ethics.

Bone, flesh, oil—indifference
if interest compounds.

Once, in a dream, your kin
midcut sensed human,
sliced tender, hurried but keen,
and I before I even knew
I'd be I came groggy:
"Glory, glory, glo—"

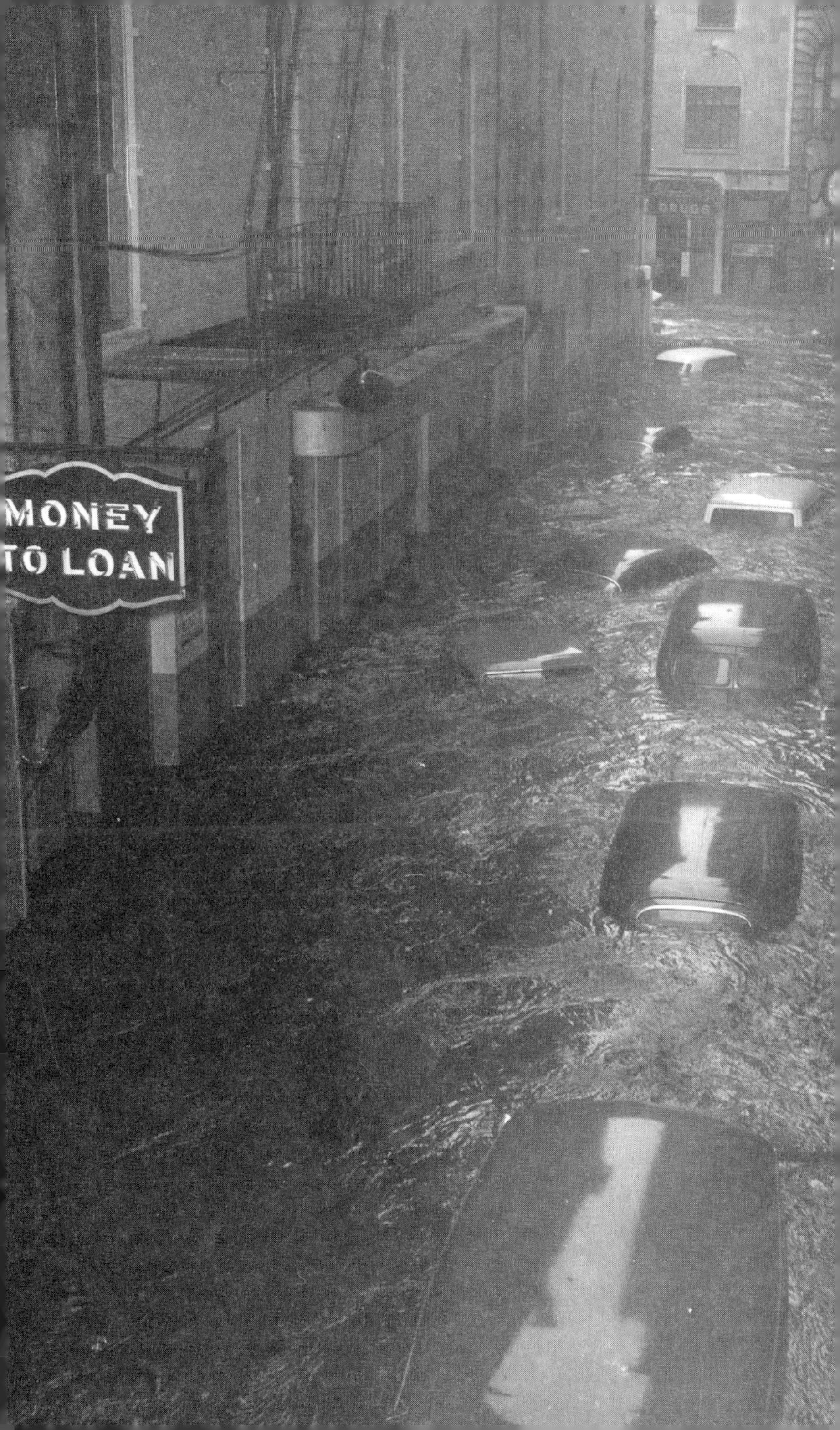
MONEY
TO LOAN

Trouble on the
Road Again

Tucked back (even prints have sculleries)
poles skulk on silver, ideograms of slash,
crack, hoisting; spray-can slang for *post*.

All this water free for sacramental
using in this state with Plantation
in its name yet no warner's voice
keens up to say come baptize
this place again, let our great-great-great-
grandchattel carry on.

Foreground, futures wade car-mired,
concocting coming through.

Legend

Full and ripply—supple
like you had no bones
you swashed down main street
naked and they watched.
In pics you're thick and muddy.
Gossip had it you were loud.
Seriously show out like that
in Georgia you would cue
good blues. But upsouth
has no love for thick dark women
busting out.

What if I write a lyric? Witness falsely?
Just go sprawling with the truth?
Sing I saw your chattahooching?
How you ran this town.

Aftermath

Gel tears film my corneas.
No contacts in yet. Life blurs.

I need to quit-back coffee.
This print I look at nose-to-paper
in the waiting trembles like a sail,
stuttering canvas, or a polaroided
fan up into color out of gray.

Bless the SX-70. Fold-up-fold-down
thing so yoga origamic. Quick snap
and a cartoon-flattened insect
is a camera come to life.

I'm half dissolved to Kingston,
maybe '72, tooling some neighbor's
cousin's neighbor's camera
in our small well-planted yard.

Short pants for age and not weather.
I'm shooting made-up soldiers
in a TV-triggered war—lime tree
armored spiky, hardwood almond

satellited with green patrolling eyes,
the acerola's set-off squibs stoke color.
Dog perks. I wag prints.

Then inside in storm season when
sun would hit and hold a vocable,
diminish it to palms-together leaves
and we'd tuck in from porch and batten,
flabbergasted mongrel too; no current;
louvers tight as hatches; outside rumoring
like war; caught water rationed; the candles
for the duppy dem eked out, mine always
at-the-ready ratchet knives.

Lenses in now. Vision up. Outside, a mill,
a village and a valley thick with conifers
made plaid by window grids. The print steadies,
agitation fixed.

Who can miss the lintels? Brows astonished.
History hidden in plain sight—that repeated
adventitious Irish name and then people!
People. Jeezam. People. Tall-set in the windows.
Brows and pupils. Eyes.

What does the hurricane teach us?

The house locked like a theater,
my senses on alert and me projecting—
passing time. My siblings maybe
doing their own mysterious things.
The boom of blown pawpaws
fashioned cannons, genies came from
zinc sheets sailing whoosh, the wind's pitch
of furnace dragonned. When a cable fell it hissed.

Aftermath. To boy who shot Polaroids:
counting every blessing after wrath was done.

Picturebook Brockton

The subject matter is so much more
important than the photographer.
—Gordon Parks

(i) Ready

(*said the man with the handsewn lapels*)

Folks like me are always ready.
Time bogarts, barges, just comes.
I've got freight in the system,
nod to cargo, dap up trucks.

Free, I move cool, arms snug
straight or crossed. Don't provoke,
appeal neither. Appeal and you're
ballistic. On just errands I suit,

lotion, T-blade my temples,
get hair hedged off. Every bye ma
rehearsal. Dignified for view.
Put together decent for the shot.

(ii) *Espoleta*

(for the woman with the red carry-on)

First look a month ago I fashioned her
an aesthete, focused on the lance-point boots,
the teal skirt hem-flouncy, magenta jumper
streamed on by black hair. This time, it's her *where*
that draws me: short porch of trey-decker,
siding-clad facade behind her, grille columns either side.
Does this iron feel embarrassed, go corroding quicker
when she flies from Massa landlock,
soars Florida to *canela* and *clavos de olor*
and balconies so rococo there's no need to know
rococo's meaning. Its basic sound astounds.
And the water where she earned her *grinn carr*
—blue rivers, lily-appliquéd ponds, bay waves
drenching sand impaled by self-relighting matches, *palmas*;
the languages *indios* weave from conquest,
the clichéd Galician cadence—silly affectation
of her dad. Cropped as is, the image makes it hard
to say if the scrolly posts are frivolous or work elements.
The constancy of looking blurs decision.
Sounds insightful, but come on, is this true?

The body I see this time well, it weighs on me . . .
the toddling suitcase, suitcase husky child,
me and my mother, her grip on me at soon-waist-height
already inches loose. Close stranger, I pray you fortune.
   —And I like your face. Did I say this?—
cheekbones lifting wide from chin point, *pera*,
winging *espoleta*, true vee shape. When you smile,
I know you crack it. Good luck, Wishbone.

(iii) Star

(for the man in the star-spangled blankie)

Lumumba look-alike, your gaze urges,
"Whisper Whitman," poet of tumult,
seer of waves. Last night I had a beard again
and in his body on a bridge uttering
through his spatter prophetics,
vowels mossy, whiskers crashed on face.

Star, I can't remember poems and my own
are best reneged. Erratum! Wasn't Walt
in my dim dreaming, it was Burning Spear,
Isaiah re-astonished to life by demigods
in electromechanical counsel at their fader-ready
boards, blues infused and reggae arrogant.

Power in politics is construction.
In music we redoubt.

Somewhere in the world on the night of your trip
to this imperial Hollywood promise,
Roman candles strafed a sky like when a kiss
comes in old films and clouds get raunchy-splurge.

Folks ate sauced-on tubers, *boofed* roots;
contrails paused before unravel
got praise like tripe in goat head soup,
kudos like a long unspooling solo
from Tom Varner's French horn.

So, red white and who?

Whitman: *To me, every hour of the day is
an unspeakably perfect miracle.*

Spear: *If I walk away from music, I walk
away from myself.*

(iv) Lough

(for the granddad at the blow-up pool)

And then there comes that step when grands
hitch, recusp on child. In this interstice, baptismal
waters and the camphor bath of corpses join one.
It's as when one sees the stalk of a neglected
croton just before it ramifies from luck or care,
or the tease of headwaters through the variegated
shadows of the woods, a negligee so subtle
it meshes with the mind, casting over it church lore
and parable logic. And here he is, blotchy guard angel
at a Brockton lough—skin wings slung from arms,
leagues from Eire roosting, grand-boy in the backyard.
Allow him cherub sword.

IV

Barn

From a plastic Adirondack on the back deck
of a cabin sealed once but abandoned
to a splinter-shaggy-cinder-silver-gray,
I'd watched day diminish as vision does
when force on eye nerve bloats (vignetting)
and I'd come through regimented grass,
curt-sleeved, legs mosquito peppered
as guest mates in the big house
drowsed on pét-nat and edibles.

      Around me swirling glowworms toked.

An ocher dinner party in a skylight-debossed
new buy, a teardown-put-back in bland exurbia
where almost mansions had been set up on extinguished
farms, the relics of failed effort scenic: frog ponds,
wells and meadows, barns and wallsteads
and what conscious double-work it took to get here
in capital's late-stage *now*.

In the barn under shadow-vined beams
in an inbetween of Worcester-and-Boston evening,
I sensed a hovering *then*, thing or moment

wanting, a calling down, a pulse in third
iris, unwell strobe with flaps as cranky
as the old barn doors left gulled with
every eke of effort bringing cringe.

The night before, unspooling like a scarf
or *flimm*, a dream as locomotive as a flush
of Muybridge cards—

My steeplechasing mind at gallop leaped—
dolphins in a spindrift as a dugout plowed
the billows off a coast, a coast not where I'm from,
shore with cast of say the Comoros, Mauritius,
beenie—not bounty Madagascar,
more like say Seychelles, and still the hills
there knew me as a bredrin unaligned,
and they stood off, judging, all lava-thick
with woods, clannish in their grouping,
allocentrics—till *zoop*—a contrast cut
to gravy boat, and me swamped
at supper in a house I dimly knew
splashed in fish broth, arms thyme kelped
while SOSing rice *djahazis*,
yam tugs and spatchcock catamarans;
all this under a saber-billed bananaquit,
at least it's what I thought, eggset
in a bronze drum chandelier
and no kin there, no guests, just settings.

I woke up broken, slow-came-to
in riled up percale, drained and draining
as war mares lost of riders broke on me,
cavalcade all leathergone, lapis
tumbling on the reef.

Conundrum.

What is *then* and then this now?

Past the bare dirt stalls with their flopped hinges,
my nose hairs eyelashing waked dust, talcum
of solace for the plain pine boards,
I took the slim and rail-less stairs to the hayloft,
the riddim of my Wallabees *splat*; up there,
music from the drink up started faltering
through the left apart doorwindows wherethrough
drylife was once flung, tender soft-shoe,
maybe Coles and Atkins, or ponies
on a leaf embroidered road, a sweet sound
trampled roughshod by a spurred-on train,
a gyre-thunder airing westish in the woods,
a pitch of equus in the electromechanics
of painbray, liturgical horror groan,
wheel cut after wheel cut on the keloid rails.

Oh Jah Rastafari what's become of me?

I easied to the hoistdown window
as the longtail locomotive counterfaded
other way and the frog pond went choric
as the Sonos in the big *revitallated* house
let go of the palpitating hand of old maracas,
kaiso, and out came the cut glass tone
of a piano fingered tentative
the way neuropathy from sugar
makes the foot phalanges linger on each
floorboard for the feel . . . console . . .
Thelonious . . . good nickname for folks like me
who call themselves apart and take the risk
and implications of eccentrics, hell-bent
go-iters alone.

I looked out across the tree line yards away—
the toothy block of it—a band of clouds
were closing down, and thinking filled:
this like-this is what the Jonah bredrin
glimpsed at from the mouthparts of the whale.

A-framed ark of the covenant!

I looked up and saw in truss and stanchion
ribbed figuration of what choosing loose belonging
could have wrought, what life coulda
favor if your promise was shook,

if I'd cast myself from grace and off
my kilter, flipped up, ended upside down,
and I confessed I had, admitted all the goodness
in my life was undeserved.

On the walk back to the cabin for the succor
of my drink, from there thankful to the backsteps
of the jazz-lit house, I let mosquitoes scourge me,
leave me riddled like I do when actors rough me
from the stage, and I imagined what it must have
been for those yoke-and-collar-casted horses
in this gasping soil, frost and damp winters.

Did they, like us in our barracks
dream fleeing, sense possible and parable
in trains, rear up two-footed in event of?

> As if?
> Practice human or,

> or say centaur. Two-handers.

Each night
sheep booed.

Mons of Luke Al Dente

Basil from a pot on the veranda,
overpriced pinoli and pimientos
pressured into dust, brassy olio
from TJ's rumored virgin, Greek alleged,
Israeli sea salt from Whole Foods
and Parmigiano-Reggiano
from that shoppe in Wayland Square
where la señora with the Spanish-speaking
helper and the bum preserved by lunges
reaches from her core for briny lemons,
Brie, sausage and taut ficelle flow in
from Orly and loose tea.

To pestle proper is a patience.
Squelching herbs and oil without no spillage
stone to stone is zazen for the savage,
koan in practice, jag belief.

If you did *deh-yah* babylove I woulda feed you,
fess up to the slipup with the garlic
as we lapse in chairs out-folded on the pout
projecting from this brick face building
where in daytime June-tucked herbs
in earthen gardens get full dandy for the sun.

If you did *deh-yah* babylove yours would be
bow ties pesto-dyed. Bow ties and Torrontés,
Mendocino short of gelid, pampas golden sipped in spate.

That slab table from the TIFF you joked off
as "enbuttered with thick books" I am there now,
taking succor in a mons of luke al dente
as I doodle and address pink Post-its like postcards.

I mammer to your belly's earhole
as you do your what-you-do there
in your way-off near-far town.

Did you think a year would pass
before I got the what of what you wrote of
of the lemons? How when fixed in salt
they tang the tongue?

Tonight I cleared a spot, annulled my mustache.

Have a bow tie.
Let this salt and sour wince you.

Spring a nib of pee.

All the Kin-ness
in Foil Shrouds

You called tilapia snapper's cousin.
King fish? In-law-like to shark.
You styled Jamaicans zealous
with ginger, lax to mash allspice.
Good *bad* though with soup
but all-you do provisions clumsy—
yam ent cut up like the meat.

Jan love, now you're silent
braising in respect, hat-lidded,
eyes in owlish glasses
sclerotic wings crisscrossed.

True gran, nomad for de youth-dem,
gypsy-cabber to track meets, recitations,
sweetie cupboard in the purse.

We hush toward your casket,
file the wooden pews *sotto* organ *voce*,
cane field riddim thudding out.

When God dished you Gehrig's
you took worship for the halt
and staycd the hobble,
said the drugs would make you dunce
now here you lie in garnish,
room reserver at the motor inn checked out.

If I go to the after-banquet
I may toast you, gourmandize
while ruing, nod thanks for cou-cou
warm when offered, all the kin-ness
in foil shrouds—roti skins
transparent caskets I'll leave with,
the odor of belonging in my hair,
prick crown of jerk, of curry,
of escoveitch and gungo,
of sorrel and white rum.

Mother of my no longer wife
death vexes. Long to fight with you.

Boy—bigger cock than you
does crow and end up in pelau.

New Kingston

Poolside. Summer. Sixties-style hotel. Blocky cutout
of the modern in a thought-out business zone.

New Kingston. Second take on commerce set up
midway to the hills. Far from slum and harbor.

Far from prison and court. Far from market where
goats skin out in public for the curry and the drum.

This poolside scene could stand for California,
deals being cut at café tables, sharp sunglasses,

white skin tinting brown. And lined along
the chaises: potted ficus, cacti, palms.

Downtown, which could play New Orleans in a movie
lean trees that keep secrets, ancient confidants of slaves,

human beings who willed their lives to pollen,
said, "Take it," as the atlas caught the noose.

On certain evenings after sunset grains of hazing yellow
crack and duppies saunter out, float-linger on the yuck

of progress: diesel, warm garbage, sinkholes of filth,
cast-off people filming with that brutal human funk.

When these grains explode inhaling stutters,
eyes and nostrils run—yes, this does occur—

and centuries and centuries of loss come back as odors,
memos from the limbic, scents of what the outpost

ranked as vital, needed, vetted, listed, ordered,
planned for, brokered, lashed below for months:

burlap, buckshot, barrels, powder, niggers, cod.
In a tinny speaker in a mango tree some reggae natters.

The tree is big and afroed, strapping with whitewashing
on its trunk. What species? Tom the Wrinkly Barman

doesn't know. Quips, "It's barren." Shakes martini.
"Hasn't borne in fifty years." Ruckus slaps a branch.

Farfetching

I dream a shadow self sometimes. Last night
he was a boy eye-troubled, nearsighted
to the point he saw newsprint as dots,
so he saw the universe in fractions,
and utilized his knowing on pay-Fridays
at the docks, taking in the parlance
disadvantage of dockworkers shrunk
by gantries and red rum.

Waterfront. Prostitutes. Belly skin
with tiger stripes. Pinto mongrels.
Crown & Anchor men. His scruffed khakis.
Rayed school tie. Tampering with probables.
Dicemen charming. Arms writhe. Cups rattle.
Brine air biting focus through
cook smoke and steaming piss.

Glassed him in the huddle,
judging risk, scatting number scales
shadowmanning incidence,
surmising likely, speculating as he will
in lonesome with books he buys
from this day's profit. Almond tree,
head cooled by church fan leaves,

he hedges fake prophetic,
farfetching in the spell of new words
like he did at twelve with Gazpacho,
a 59 to 1 at Watson's which he bet on
and lost, for how could he not side
with the Apaches who marauded to the steppes
to pitch tents with Cossacks? And who would
waste a name like that on soup?

He lies here now in half-light
without contacts and his light gray
flat is all amush with birdcalls
and the vinaigrette smell of caked wine.
I see him acappelling for relevance
in the house whose wanting haunted,
his prayed hurt sui generis as one
below a vinculum that slabs a fat amount.

In this big house by himself
he reads rejections, trades without brokers,
plays pickup cricket on a grass court
with old spars and grows sensi
for capricious melanoma
next to heirloom Black Krims
grown out of seeds sown in
glow days when awrightish husband
and good poet were the picks to win.

Twice a week he blends his own gazpacho,
half Heart of Compassion, half canned
and slurps its metacool, bones porous,
all flesh like my balls.

Great Apache fighters of the Cossacks,
promise sound will save, say no
consequence will come from dreams.
Let me to be child. Holler back.

The Vendor of New Hearts

Me? Once way-far in time in a village coiled from stone
I met an elder in a teahouse. He proposed, and I said yes
I'll join you, and we walked together to the vendor of new hearts.

I bought one, an olive, a fat one, did as I was told,
set it on my soft chest near where my birthmark is
and when I flew home and kissed my children

one sniffed up "dandelion" and the other hmmmmd "wild grass."
A friend said since that trip I give my time more easy,
that my "my-bads" and "sorrys" have a ghee-ish butter feel.

Look, you're the friend who said I share time freer, so you
know the olive worked; so my dear one, as I sit here
at your bedside consoling while you sweat out in your

nightgown-jellied grief, let me choose. For you,
a sweet-tart pomegranate, *prongonat*, combo lung and heart,
efficient pumper for the hiccup sobs to come.

It's even lovelier when broken—and whole?—thug-tough
and unlike evie's red delicious, when slit does not air-brown.
Friend, why wouldn't you want to have in you

self-parable, hive of glammy seed coats just embedded
not stuck? I should tell you as you brow-twitch in this dim room's
lily smell babes, when a new hub starts its sink-in, fuck it burns

and coughing up the old one with its huck pneumonics isn't nice,
but the godheart can't live through abscission. How it goes, I've
    heard,
you're out part-fine then brown anthurium leaf drops on your shoe.

Glaze Eyed at the
Humble Shapings

Halfway from Kingston to
Watchwell, Vauxhall convoy
smoking like a navy in retreat,
they took the swell of foothills

cutting door-high mist,
everyone black in skin and cloth
and late-sixties gendered:
girls decked in mantillas,

boys aunt-rigged in ties.
There below cool Mandeville
she glimpsed an elder half-emergent from
a hut pitched in palm shags,

rod legs in nappy-slack briefs,
rope arms round what to her
carsick six-self was a giant's
dull brass goblet or a godlet's

broke brown egg. Now
on runabouts to Watchwell
in her Necchi-putting Volks
she leaves bypass, stitches village,

sweet-foots the downshifts
and toots. She and dready drift
in smoke through clay wreckage
to a jumbo yabba like the one

she glimpsed that way-far time.
They cup out soup to *apakyi*.
Their habit half-quiet
chew-slap and blow

do talk as they gaze
glaze-eyed at the humble shapings,
holding still, performing,
ringed by white-hot coals.

Potter, plaiter of myths
more pliant than the stickles
of your ribs and listing hut—
raj remnant, sadhu look-alike,

twice in dreams she kissed your
ginger foot and stroked your dreadful
unconditioned hair in thanks
for kilning Africa to life.

Sometimes she wonders if you
hear her sweet-foot and tooting
on the distant bypass with the
trucks and compact automatics

on the days she doesn't
come, or if you understand in man's
language that each time
she doesn't take the ruts

along the main her convoy sailed on to
mourn her granddad's death in Watchwell
that way-far time, it's she who sends
the dogs and goats to tack as if aimless

past your rock reef of made stone
to that horseshoe of crabgrass
at the lank door where you greet them
uplifted palms claystubborned,

posture like an oracle's, eyes tinted
turmeric with burnt-in disillusion
for the souls dem gone tinnish
while you work the weight.

In Fuguing Wake

(Amy Clampitt, for you)

Casual. Flitting skin off cucumbers over
a wide metal bowl, catcher for the harvest
from the summer market, that cosmos
of virtue—jug bands, frailed banjos, picked
mandolins, tomatoes as a toddler sees them,
mitts of stars—I feel a comet trail of shiver
where my sternum is, that bone high school
posters flat out to a Roman sword, but
dug up horrors prove as dropping bombs.

I know it's nothing serious, which worries.
I'm known to be pulled along and flipped
in fuguing wake. It's good this happened at the sink,
at evening, with time before the white flock orchestra
descends the grass drifts through the shrub maze
of picnickers and their pickneys on Tanglewood's
lawn. Shed bound! Music in hand and jaw muscles;
the old estate spellcast as something sacral near
Kripalu's mount where stone hips cleave.

I'll be there in the back with maples, oaks or birches,
X-legged with Txakolina for as long as I can bear,

cut jeans on the blue quilt gifted by a poet from Oaxaca
to embrace my then small children when I wasn't
home and here I am not home again, months here
in this cottage in this rumple-range terrain,
summer homestead of phantasmal ease: Shakespeare
by starlight, Martha Graham's wraithings,
mill blood museums, high-priced downward dogs,

and all year, inns in mansions, British-eyed
manors, valleys with asemic oratory
patterned with what private cars elided
from Manhattan—big gauge rail.
Once, I swashed about a bend as if in winter
on a sled, found origin: a high rock face
bird-ferned, no curb just bushing then
road so thin my silver comet must have
singed that low stone fence stacked

with logic like dry wood, marker for the sheer
fall to an olive river chilling twenty feet
below, just lazy, just shiftless, not wanting to
be Hudson or Mackenzie, Zambezi, Ob,
Huang He, Purus or Nile, unambitious but
with hint in watermark it often spites, cussing
sotto voce like my petty Rio Grande does
through what we scale-exempt Jamaicans call a gorge.
Look good in the bushing—the bevel cut for rail.

This flesh in its not-green greenness
comets me in slow arc to a beach in Anguilla,
a place rolled and sprinkled with hotels,
empire's latest quest. Cane nor cotton
rooted here despite keratoconic oversight:
Oh the whipped when healed have keloids,
so the catting doesn't work so well if those
who love them don't know braille.
Bless fingerprints (we tell our food by skin).

In this eel island's shallows, the skin of recollection
peels, everts leisure, flips the calendar of ease.
Winter is Antillean frolic season. Here, August blisters
quick-quick in air too damn sun-strong. The combers
by the like-it's-Eid-in-the-Sahara-by-religion-closed hotel
obscene. My swim wake churns the clear-clear
surf. To translucence it is spoiled. Who dreamed
this, this shiver of villas, prompts of fins . . .
this pastiche of lateen sails? Good stranding here. Alone.

It feels ablative. Is there such a word?
I'm shy to pare my clothes. Though I understand
this multilingual archipelago as accident . . .
tectonics, coral . . . science . . . *moosh* and *voof*;
though I know plumb flight from here to
my own island's all-inclusive-cuffed north coast
is nine hundred mash-mash miles, I feel indulgent,

touristic, bathing naked here in Windsor Castle's sea.
Is it politics? Asemics? Ghost marks on my skin?

There's heat etch on my corneas as I drift
purse eyed, slow turn in this gourd flesh tinted
sea as cool as—each cliché is intaglio
and there's always room and need to shave—
as cool as . . . as cool as, as cool as one can be
while getting palmed by that translucence one rasps,
is frilling longwise into waves collapsing in a
wide bowl in the Berkshires, basin-filled hill province
of the baronesque, of countryfolk and writers:

Hawthorne, Wharton, Melville, Du Bois.
In this unremodeled kitchen cooked
a modest poet of indecent skill, Clampitt
who bloomed late and in profuse
language, her labyrinths from this simple
home breath-hitching as the gardens
Beatrix Jones Farrand baroqued for
Wharton at The Mount.

For now and months to come I'm Berkshire too.
I'm bass lake, escarpment stroll, bay horses
grazing long necked, red barn on the rise;
as well the grandfathered split-rail fence,
facets glinting, the village with the lancing church,

the felt common. I'm the hulled town
streetpill-glumed; the plein air philharmonic,
the market bounty-gemmed, the—
did a fox skurch by my window or a cat?

On a hike a black dog rushed me while
its owners stayed off pace and I knew
I'd kick it if it lunged and it did and I did not.
A statement is a story, a salad of precisely
mandolined ingredients, dressed up;
and what if I were celeried, mustarded,
mayonnaised? Things I do not like.
At Tanglewood, mosquitoes will chorus,
picnickers will gnat and I will camp

on my *alfombra*, the story of me here
saladed, tremble like a kite on sound's
current, belly in halfing light to galactic fireflies,
the cosmos, way-far up in the stuttering
consolations, swoon, the shake at breastbone
in the kitchen the work of self-yeast
as much as sparked comet, a rise to infinite
in gratitude, forgiveness, in terror, in faith,
high as a cello in the red realm. Liszt.

Acknowledgments

Acknowledgments are warmly extended to the editors of the following, where some of these poems have appeared: *The Atlantic*, *The New Yorker*, *The Poetry Review*, *Agni*, *Conjunctions*, *Harvard Review*, *Virginia Quarterly Review*, *Prairie Schooner*, *The Common*, *Liberties*, *Ruminate*, *The Wolf*, *Capitals: A Poetry Anthology* (Bloomsbury, 2017) and the *Ocean State Review*.

The photograph (details) on pages i, iv, and 123, from Karol Kozlowski Premium RM Collection / Alamy Stock Photo, is of the Black Ark Studio's ruins. The Ark was built and operated by the iconic Jamaican producer Lee "Scratch" Perry, a mentor to Bob Marley and one of the major innovators of dub. The photographs in part II are from the archives of the Providence Athenæum. The poems in part III are loose, speculative portraits in consideration of images shot by Mary Beth Meehan.

This book was completed with the support of Brown University's Henry Merritt Wriston Fellowship and Richard B. Salomon Faculty Research Award. A six-month residency at the Amy Clampitt house in the Berkshires gave me some re-zeroed time to fritter. Books take time to cook.

Personal, groundational thanks to Kwame, Ishion, Greg, Forrest, Hennessy, Janet, Cayley, Laird, Shenoda, Tricia, Kevin, Cole and Rick.

Phyllis, my mother, you taught me well: "Ingratitude is really worse than witchcraft."

Jonathan Galassi and Katie Liptak, a hug with very long arms.

Chase Twichell and Russell Banks, forever love. Peaches and Mayte. Ahhhh.